Copyright © 2020 by Aften Locken

All rights reserved. No part of this book may be reproduced or used in any manner without written permission of the copyright owner. The exception would be in the case of brief quotations embodied in the critical articles or reviews and pages where permission is specifically granted by the publisher or author.

FIRST EDITION

For my Mister Man:
No matter what I've weighed, you always insisted I was only either skinny or less skinny.

Contents

Where We've Gone Wrong and Where to Go Now	1
Change Your Mind Before Your Body	10
Play Dress-Up	15
No More Numbers	18
If Ya Got It Flaunt It	19
Summary of Tools	24
The Only Rule You'll Ever Need for Eating	26
What's for Dinner? Anything	28
Give Your Body Some Cred	31
Whenever's Clever	37
This is How We Chew It	39
Bottoms Up	47
Summary of Tools	50
Weight-Life Balance	52
Delete Deprivation	53
Hello, Hunger	54
Live in Harmony	56
Summary of Tools	62
Exercise and Other Good-for-You Stuff	64
Fitness for (Real) Life	65
Refresher Course	73
You-ness	75
Summary of Tools	76
Comprehensive Summary of Tools	78

Where We've Gone Wrong and Where to Go Now

Everyone wants to be thin. The thing is, to be thin you're going to need to lighten up! Literally and in your pretty, little head. With this method, you will learn ways to see yourself and food as pleasures to be enjoyed. The result is gradual, realistic and delightful weight loss that is yours for life.

I'm not a dietitian, medical professional or a personal trainer. I am a real person who lives a real life. I have struggled with real body issues just like you. Thankfully, I found real solutions, which I will share with you. For ten years, I battled eating disorders of every kind that eventually left me completely removed from my sense of self, totally clueless on how to eat normally and overweight. My view of my body and food was more than just a touch out of whack.

As a kid, I wasn't off to a great start anyway. My dear, sweet mother had already had a tough time of it. Her parents, although likely well-meaning, started her on a diet at eight years old. Needless to say, my mother hadn't really felt okay about herself since...well, ever. My stepfather was a devoted health nut, all about raw foods and homeopathy, way before that stuff was cool. The result was a household cuisine that was bland and cold, and where sugar was regarded like some kind of neurotoxin.

I didn't have weight problems as a youngster, less a chubby phase right before puberty that stretched me out into a long, lean teenager. Still, my young mind was vulnerable, easily allowing anorexia to take root there. (Yes, I've had daddy issues too, in case you were wondering.) Despite my naturally slender build, I became convinced I was fat and subsisted on impossibly minimal amounts of food, which wasn't nearly enough to handle the hours of frenzied, daily exercise.

A few years into that masochism, the disease morphed into bulimia as I became obsessed with all of the food I had been denying myself. And I'm talking even super typical food—like toast. Once I toasted an entire loaf of bread, only to make myself sick and continue the cycle. I became so consumed with my illness, I had to drop out of college. There wasn't any room in my head to focus on other things. More years with that behavior passed. The purges eventually dropped off as I became fully consumed with compulsive overeating. I tried diet after diet, forcing myself to conjure up the same crazed discipline I used to starve myself before. I failed every single one.

I visited a few doctors and tried some therapy, both with a psychologist and a couple of nutritionists. I got nothing out of the psych therapy, except a lot of expensive bills. There was a doctor who prescribed an exact calorie count I should take in each day. Basically, a diet. One nutritionist was convinced she had cured me after six weeks and told me I didn't need to come back.

Spoiler alert. I was not cured.

Another nutritionist once gave me an excerpt to read about what "normal eating" was like. The description sounded so wonderful and so far out of reach from where I was that I burst into tears as I read it. Beyond that, her work with me was not very effective. I spent ten whole years this way. In the end, I found myself without a clue about how to really eat, wholly hating my ravaged body and overweight.

Overfed, underfed and everything in between, I finally got fed up. A switch flipped and I saw food, eating and my body and myself in completely new light. Shining, sparkling, happy lights—like a disco dance floor, complete with a glittering, mirrored ball. I went from "I'm a chubby, ugly worm," to "Damn, girl. Me sexy." And that was before I'd even lost an ounce.

The weight loss came with tools I developed and finessed for eating, exercise and finding a balance. These tools are realistic, practical and not crazy. Through trial and error, I have fine-tuned them for myself, and am happy to say I have since spent the last ten years actually living an amazing life. That and I am way, way less fat. (I've even been labeled as skinny.) Now these tools are written out clearly for you in this nice, little, bite-sized book.

But enough about me—let's talk about YOU!

Perhaps you, at some point in your past, wanted to lose some weight and a diet innocently seemed like the right solution. Maybe it even worked. For a while, that is. Yet, all too quickly, even the slightest intake of regular foods seemed to render weight gain again. Because you had success before, you go for it again, you persistent, willful, darling thing. Victory! You lost the weight.

But, wait—what's this? A few little slip-ups and your pants don't fit? That does it! Never again! You really mean it this time. Well...starting Monday...and after this weekend out with the girls. No, it's going to have be the week after that. You'll be out of town and it's too hard to find the right diet foods when traveling. You know, work has been a killer. But once it calms down, *then* you will get back to it.

Try as you might, the dieting and your best intentions just can't seem to make the weight loss stick. But you're smart, capable and you just know that if you could only get yourself to commit to this next one, your weight problems would be solved. It's not you, sweet cheeks. It's the diet.

Maybe your food wars have waged since childhood. If you had a parent who modeled controlled eating, your relationship with food may be muddled, at best. It isn't easy making peace with all foods, when you grew up learning it was something to be counted and measured and withheld. What's worse is feeling the same way about your body. Especially for us ladies, having a mother who forever criticized her looks can send a clear message. You may have learned to question the value of your own physical appearance, pointing out any perceived flaw as a force to be reckoned with. I sincerely hope this pattern can stop and not be passed on to daughters, the women of the future.

Even if you haven't marched along a dieting parade, or eating wasn't a big deal when you were a kid but you still are having weight trouble, this book is for you. Let's face it: Food. Is. Everywhere. There are restaurants, deliveries and cuisines of every kind. It seems like no one can walk a block without being confronted with tasty snack options. The key to losing and managing weight for life is not about denying yourself those things. It is learning to live harmoniously and enjoyably with them.

What you are going to explore here starts with a mindset. You will be finding a balance that is unique to you. This is a guide. It's not some woo-woo meditation, mindfulness, modern-hippy mantra. It promotes an attitude adjustment that is supplemented with practical, applicable tools and tips that you can really use. These are the tangible tidbits you can hold on to. I think one reason we like traditional diet plans is they are very easy to grasp in our logical minds. This program feeds that rational side, with tools and tips, and the mindful side with a conceptual method. It allows you to move through the fluctuations of life, while consistently keeping yourself and your body balanced.

Before I got my act together in the eating department, I could only look at a bag of candy—my most favorite, delectable, irresistibly chow-down-able candy (Twizzlers)—as my arch nemesis. A war would wage in my mind over that bag of sticky delight, one I would inevitably lose. In my defeat, I would ravage the entire bag, not enjoying a single bite, as I slumped further into self-loathing. Nowadays, that same bag of candy poses absolutely no threat, which still amazes me. I can just as easily enjoy some as I can shrug and disregard it. Either way, I don't gain weight.

Here, you will not find a list of good foods and bad foods. There are no workout routines. No diets. I may make some references to what I eat or how I exercise, but this is not intended to be copied. This is a perspective. A way of thinking that helps you make your own best decisions of what to eat and how to exercise. There are no formulas or lists or routines to be replicated here. Numbers don't apply. You don't weigh yourself. You don't track when you should or shouldn't eat. You don't even see the word "healthy," because I feel it's too staunch and formal. Instead, you will see "lean" and "heavy" as descriptors for food. Those terms feel more approachable and easier to digest. (Plus, it's grammatically incorrect to say food is healthy. The adjective is healthful. I know, I know, I can't help it. When I did go back to finish college, I majored in journalism.) This book is made to be short and sweet and to the point.

If what I say and how I say it resonates with just one other person and it helps them, I have succeeded. My struggles with myself and lessons learned have been worth it. Maybe some of the information you get here can also be found in other weight loss programs. That's great! Repetition is key to learning. I am not claiming a breakthrough, revolutionary method. I am simply explaining to you what I have found works for me for over a decade. Sometimes we need the same information said a certain way for it to click, or it's the way someone says that same thing that it suddenly makes sense. Other times, we are just ready to listen to what we have been hearing all along. That's why we need each other, for new perspectives when we can't get out of our own heads.

I implore you to bring only two things with you as you begin. The first is—excitement! Think of any time you've lost weight in the past how elated you felt. Dropping pounds feels amazing. You feel confident and energized. That is the sensation you may have from start to finish and beyond in this weight loss journey. It's not reserved only for the fleeting end result. Bottle up some of that buzzing glee you remember feeling, and be ready to carry it with you.

Second, please bring your patience. This is not a quick fix. You are going for the long-term here—as in, lifelong. I am not making a promise of thirty pounds in thirty days. In my case, I lost about thirty pounds in two years. I know that may sound really slow, especially if you know your sister's wedding is coming up in three months and you want to blow some minds in the pictures. Trust me, honey, I know you will blow minds no matter what! The difference with this way of life is that I have never put the weight back on. Not even close. Relax and have fun. Your results from practicing these tools will surely differ from mine, and in a way that is best for you.

Think about it this way: Where were you with your weight two years ago? How would your life have been different if, at that time, you had started a process like this one, and now, instead of reading this introduction, you were already in a way better place with your body? A year is going to go by anyway, as is two, five or ten, as far as we know. You can keep doing what you've been doing that has brought you to this point. Or, you can follow my suggestions and give yourself a chance to lose weight gently and permanently. How many years have you spent losing and gaining weight? Do you want the next number of years to go by like that? No? That's what I thought. I can totally feel you there. Enough time has been spent on those old ways. The time to start your new way is today.

Section 1

Change Your Mind Before Your Body

The number one most important, completely critical, totally fundamental piece to this entire weight loss method is: Love your body. Exactly the way it is right now. Not twenty pounds less from now, or fifty, ten or even just five. Right. Now. This is the foundation for every other part of this weight loss method to work. It is also, perhaps, the most difficult, so don't blow over it. Don't just say, "Okay. Fine. I love my body. Yay. Now let's get on to the weight loss part."

The weight loss part starts with loving your body, before you've lost any weight. Don't freak. No matter how much you have berated your own reflection with not very nice comments that you would never dream of saying to a friend, it can be done. Plus, there's a gosh darn good reason for it. Think about it. Have you ever planned to lose weight with a mindset of, "I freaking adore myself and I'm madly in love with my body that deserves all the wonderful things. I'm going to treat myself to some weight loss"? Probably not. We "treat" ourselves by taking a spoon to a bucket of ice cream, many times as a reward for putting up with some miserable weight loss regimen, fueled by self-loathing.

Diets often start solely because we hate the way we look. We respond by subjecting ourselves to restriction and deprivation, harshly slapping our own wrists whenever we reach for something to make the pain stop. What's worse is that no one is alone in this. This kind of self-inflicted torture seems normal. Go up to just about anyone and say, in that familiar tone of woeful sarcasm with a sigh, "The diet starts tomorrow." You'll likely receive an understanding groan, both of you bonding in a knowing eye roll of how awful it is.

Now think about this. Has it worked? The very obvious answer is no, or you wouldn't be reading this. I too was once a sympathetic eye roller who did all the same not nice things to myself to be thin. At long last, thank all the goddesses, I realized self-hatred wasn't getting me any thinner and that maybe it was time to play nice. It didn't feel good to hate myself. It must be flipped around. Love your body first. Loving your body leads to caring for your body, which leads to losing weight, which cycles back to loving your body. It goes on forever and ever, like some kind of heavenly carousel.

The first time I discovered how effective this love-your-body business could be was a total accident. After ten years of brutal eating disorders, my twisted mania had left me exhausted, unfulfilled and carrying thirty extra pounds. Yup. That's what I got for spending my existence fretting over food, calories, pounds, inches and dress sizes. And believe me, I was damn good at it. If there was ever a fleeting moment that went by not consumed with these thoughts it was spent hating the way I looked. I wound up fat anyway.

In that place, feeling like a walrus, it all seemed so pointless. I had been spinning my wheels only to wind up exactly where I didn't want to be: overweight and miserable. Obviously, I couldn't control my weight. All of that time was wasted for a lost cause, but perhaps I could at least do something about the misery. I asked myself this question: What if exactly how my body is right now is how it's going to be the rest of my life?

There were two possible responses. The first was to agonize and resign myself to a life of doom, never to be enjoyed. For, no matter what I did in this world, it wouldn't be good enough. I was still fat. I was living by a long-repeated thought pattern: In order for me to have good things, I had to alter myself first. As soon as (insert weight loss goal) then I can (insert life enjoyment activity).

Well, I was way overdue for any life enjoyment activity.

The second choice was to accept my body, learn to appreciate and love what I had, and live a good—no, fan-freaking-tastic—life anyway. So I answered that pivotal question with the second response. (Phew!) For the first time, I started accepting what I had, started living and—get this—started losing weight effortlessly. This became the beginning of my weight loss journey.

Flash forward another decade to today. I am happy to say my weight loss journey has been dynamic, productive and adventurous! As an added bonus, I have remained lean and in shape, completely free from dreadful weight loss plans. Sure, I sometimes gain and lose a couple of pounds here and there. Everyone does, but it's not the drastic weight fluctuation problem I had in the past. Overall, I have spent a long time living free from weight issues, instead of spending a long time trying to be free. I will show you everything I did to have this. You are getting real tools here, but to use them properly you need to learn how to love your body. It's like being handed a set of nunchucks but you need to go to ninja school first. You must learn to be a love-your-body ninja. Even after years of thinner bliss, I often need to take a refresher course here. My mind can slip right back into old ways of thinking. I try using my weight loss weapons, but they are not effective until I get back to accepting my body first.

Perhaps all this embrace-your-shape talk sounds a bit like a platform in the body positivity movement. "What's the body positivity movement?" asks the darling you, who chooses to stray from social media. It is, much as it sounds, a popular culture motion and challenge to change mental perspectives. Viewing all body types as acceptable, it has made mega waves on social media in recent years. Search the hashtag #bopo and you will find millions of posts encouraging this radical idea, many of them delightfully heartwarming.

There is a lot to advocate for this trend of accepting all varieties of human life forms. However, that is not the focus of this book, and we won't get into any of that inner peace-y stuff. I mention it, though, because it is a very good starting point to help you with accepting and loving your current body. At the time I started my own weight loss journey, there certainly were no in-your-face campaigns about this. I'm glad there is today and I'm not one to knock in it.

I want you to please be careful, though. While I fully support the messages of this movement, I have to wonder if there is a danger in promoting overweight living. It is no secret that extra weight is a cause for health concerns. If we are sick with the flu, we don't simply accept it then do nothing to get better. We take care of ourselves and nurture our body back to health. The extra weight I once carried was a symptom of long, drawn-out physical and mental health problems. Action needed to be taken. Body positivity is a great step forward, but we will take it a step further. Love your body plus lose weight.

No one can simply read the words "love your body" and–*poof*! You magically do. It takes time, attention and practice. Here are tools for you to use.

Play Dress-Up

First, wear clothes that you look and feel your best in now. Feeling good in your clothes helps you feel good about yourself, and that's what we are going for here. So find your style.

When I started using this trick, I went with a lot of structured, sort of career-woman wear, even though I didn't really have a career. I felt totes cute in wide-leg trousers with fitted tops, jackets, sexy little vests and even hats. And, oh, was I all about pinstripes. I considered trying to pull off the adorable, curvy, pin-up girl looks with bandanas tied in my hair and bright red lipstick, but I'm just not that cool. So I went with the mafia boss lady instead.

At the time fashion was all about baby doll dresses and leggings with everything. My choices were way against the flow, but it didn't matter because I felt fabulous. Fashion is a beautiful industry, but there is no law that says we need to conform with its constant changes. It is impossible for seasonal styles to suit everybody all of the time. For example, as of this writing, current fashions have called for puffy sleeves. I have rather broad shoulders so, no matter what I weigh, puffy sleeves make me look like a football player. Never will you catch me wearing them. I can't pull off those jumpsuits everyone is into now either. They make my butt look weird.

Don't worry about the latest looks too much. These days, there are so many resources for ideas. Pinterest is a big addic...I mean, favorite of mine. I still keep boards of styles that I know work for me, one board specifically for outfits that feel cute even when I've put on a few.

Take this tool a step further and seek out fashion icons to model. Look for a body type you can relate to, and see how he or she dresses for inspiration. You may find an entire clothing brand that loves your figure. If you need a little help figuring out what to wear, give a personal styling service, like Stitch Fix, a whirl. I haven't tried it myself, but it looks pretty rad. You get to work with a stylist who helps create a look unique to you and they actually mail you stuff. So you're off the hook for ever having to go to the store. (Now that I think about it, why haven't I tried this?)

Have fun with this part! Build a wardrobe with items that make you ecstatic. Feel thrilled to pull out a pair of gorgeous boots or the most tantalizing tops for a look that is so you. You deserve to wear what makes you feel like a million gazillion bucks.

While you're re-vamping your wardrobe, get rid of your skinny jeans. I don't mean the skinny jeans style, those tapered, form-fitting pants we all know about. I mean to get rid of the jeans that you once fit into, from skinny days past. The shirts, jackets, swimsuits and everything else that no longer fits you as well. Of all the horrid afflictions I put myself through to lose weight, nothing was quite so cruel as having that teensy little crop top in the front of my closet where it taunted me.

Each day I went to get dressed, and each day I was too big to wear it. The shirt chastised me, "You wretched, worthless heifer. I will hang here and torment you every day until you force yourself to be small enough to wear me again."

Okay, so the shirt didn't actually say that. I did. To myself. But you get what I'm saying.

What I was also doing was distracting myself from happiness in the present. I was believing I was a failure because I didn't fit into those clothes. I was bombarding myself with negativity that fueled a vicious cycle of bad weight loss practices followed by inevitable weight gain. To stop it, the problem needed to be eliminated.

Get rid of everything that doesn't fit. Bag those babies up and donate them. If you're like me and have a habit of leaving donation items in the trunk of your car, driving them around and around for months, just throw them away. It's not doing you any good in your closet, and it's not doing anyone else any good in your trunk. If it's too much for you to completely get rid of the clothes, box them and place in storage. Folding them up and stacking them in a closet shelf where you can still see them, doesn't count. Out of sight out of mind applies here.

I understand wanting to keep smaller clothes around because it innocently seems like some kind of motivation to lose weight. While motivation is good, surrounding yourself with clothes that make you feel, well, fat, is not. However, this is one place where this rule can bend a tad. If it's helpful to you, keep one piece of clothing that's a size or two too small and use it as a gauge for your weight loss progress. If you are a size twelve, don't use something that's a six. A size ten would be fine. Try it on every few weeks or so, preferably on a day you're feeling fly. Experiencing your body getting closer to fitting into that item feels amazing, and that's how you want to feel all along.

No More Numbers

Another super simple tool to love your body now is to quit weighing it. I know you and your scale may have had some good days together. There may have been a time it gave you everything you wanted and made you feel beautiful, valuable and wonderful. Now whenever you get together, you leave feeling like poo. But you can't let go and keep going back to it, hoping for one more moment of validation, only to be disappointed. The romance has died. Somehow you feel like it's your fault.

Well guess what? You don't need some dumb scale to

tell you your worth. You get to feel fine all by yourself. That relationship is toxic. It's time to move on and give your loser scale das boot. Block its number. (Ha! Get it? Number?) For me, I had to break up with my measuring tape. I was obsessed with the inches of my waist, which could change with a sip of water, propelling me from feeling fine to feeling like a nervous breakdown.

Numbers are meaningless in this method. Things like your age and your weight are man-made measuring sticks that have nothing to do with the essence of you. Moving away from them is a key concept for weight loss, as you shall see. Without getting too woo woo, eating and being human are natural forces of nature. Mechanizing your daily life with numbers, like pounds or calories, will only make you feel good when you conform to someone else's idea of the right amount. Your gauge of success comes from within, based on how you feel.

If Ya Got It Flaunt It

Find your best physical feature and hone in on it with laser precision. Give that pretty-as-a-picture piece of your body all the mushy, gushy, can't-stop-stop-staring-at-myself kinda love. Have you been told you have the cutest dimples ever when you smile? Are your eyes captivating? Do you have sensational hair, an enviable booty or pretty lips? Maybe you love how tall you are or your glowy skin tone or strong arms. Find that special something about your physical self, and show it to the world like a *Honey Boo Boo* beauty pageant.

Focusing on your finest assets does two things for you. First, it works as a tool to love your body as it is. Dropping weight also means dropping the criticism of yourself and finding a thing or two, or more, about your appearance that you can really rock, is an awesome place to start. Second, it can be a focus of gratitude on those days when you are feeling not-so-sexy and need positive reinforcement.

My favey feature is a set of awesome eyebrows to grace my round little face. Granted, this lucky inheritance comes from the hairy northern European gene pool on my dad's side of the family, which also means near-constant grooming is required, from the nostrils down. Still, I love my bold brows. I meticulously groom them to maximum amazingness, bringing my confidence up with it. When I'm feeling a fat day coming on, I can get really self-conscious of my circle-shaped face. It seems to attract the first ounce of extra weight on my cheeks. Some people, I swear, can gain all kinds of weight but no one can really tell because they are able to hide it easily under clothes, while their faces look pretty much the same. Not me. If I gain even a pound it feels like half a pound goes on each cheek, and everyone notices right away. Even if this does actually happen, and it's not some crazy figment of my weird imagination, I still have my pretty brows to feel good about. Being thankful for it stops the momentum towards being mean to myself.

I think the male readers deserve something they can relate to as well, so here's an example for you fellas. I will use one of my brothers because he is totally adorable, and I know he won't sue me for writing about him. This sweet sibling of mine was always so crazy good at sports it was annoying and never dealt with weight issues. Also annoying. Then came the job and the adulting and the thirties and that changed a bit. Still, I'm quite certain no one notices his more brawny stature because no one can look past his crystal clear, pale blue eyes. He also has perfectly wavy, silky hair that looks flawless, without even trying. Even with using cheap shampoo. (Does he have any idea how much money I spend on hair products and what I, the sister, would do to have hair like that?) The point is, with a bit of manscaping, he can toss his sensational hair a bit and blink his eyes and it's all the girls around him can do to not faint. Gentlemen, you too have handsome ass assets about yourselves worth indulging in.

Whatever blessing the gene pool bestowed upon you, give it a good polish and let it shine! Just like with your style, it will help to look for actual role models possessing similar physical features like yours, for inspiration on how to rock it. Ask a friend, or someone you trust, to point some things out to you, if you're really struggling. Heck! Even if you're not struggling, ask that person to point out your hot spots anyway! It will do your confidence some good, and they might highlight a sexy you-thing you never considered before.

For far too long, I believed I was not allowed to indulge in any kind of beauty care because, even if I had a stunning hair cut, none of it would matter because my body was unacceptable, negating any effects of the improvement. Again there lay that nasty, old thought pattern. As soon as (blank) then I can (blank). As soon as I lost all of the weight then I would be allowed to be pretty.

This is a big, stinky pile of crapola! Back it up. Put this self-deprecating train in reverse. When you do things that help you look good, you feel good. When you feel good, you want to take better care of yourself, resulting in looking better and feeling better, and it cycles on upwards, until you are looking amazing and feeling your best. Give yourself permission to take an interest in your appearance now.

Color your hair to a hue that makes you feel beautiful. Whiten your teeth. Get a nose ring. Guys, groom your sexy facial hair. If Botox and fillers are your jam, go for it. My only word of caution is to not to depend on it for your full sense of self-worth, especially if you are thinking of investing in extra pricey beauty treatments. Avoid falling into that same thought pattern with different stipulations like, "As soon as I have platinum blonde hair then I will be good enough." That kind of mindset will only leave you unsatisfied and immediately searching for the next thing wrong with yourself to fix. Find a balance between acceptance and betterment.

For example, even though I am quite thin and in shape, there have been reported sightings (from myself) on my thighs of...oh god, I can't believe I'm going to admit this...cellulite. There! I said it. I hope you know how much I love you to put that out there. But it's true. I can either despair and rifle through my credit cards to see which one could withstand an uber expensive medical treatment, or I can chill out. I already do my best to take care of my body. For my legs, I started dry brushing and using a homemade body scrub with a ten dollar cream. It's enough. You know what else? I found out even supermodels have cellulite! Cellulite, ladies, is a completely normal part of being a woman and comes with all the other pretty girly bits we get to have.

Many folks will say appearance doesn't matter and it's meaningless fluff to put effort into it. That tends to be a negative comment from a narrow mindset. Personally, I think beauty and aesthetics are an under-appreciated part of life. We travel to faraway places only to gaze at some breathtaking scenery. We relax easily in spaces that are beautifully decorated. We can't help but stare at the gorgeous woman who walked in the room. It's a twist of irony that humans seem so drawn to experience beauty, then try to write it off as a shallow pursuit. Let's allow that pleasure instead of stifling it.

When I started my path to thinner bliss, before I'd lost even an ounce, I put it in my mind that I was already the size I wanted to be. I believed I was smaller, fitter, thinner now. I carried myself like I was already that size, treated myself that way, and even ate the way I envisioned thinner me would eat. I presented myself to the world with a lot more confidence. Much has been taught about positive thoughts being effective, and this is certainly a place to use that tool.

Determine for yourself the way you want your body to be, and put it in your head that it's already true. Make sure the envisioned version of you is something you can believe in. So, for example, say you've never been a size four and you can't fathom what that's like. You are probably not actually going to believe it, as much as you may tell yourself it's so. Pick a size and shape that, when you think about it, you can really feel yourself as already being that way. There will be days you struggle with believing this. To that I suggest: Fake it 'til you make it! Believe it now and one day you will wake up to find it's true.

Summary of Tools

- Love your body exactly the way it is now.
- Wear clothes you look and feel your best in now.

- Make a visual aid of your style ideas.
- Find a fashion icon with a style you can model.
- Get rid of all clothes that do not properly fit you.
- Use one piece of slightly smaller clothing to gauge your weight loss progress, every few weeks.
- Do not weigh yourself.
- Flaunt your finest physical asset(s).
- Indulge in beauty treatments.
- Believe you are already the size, shape and weight you want to be.

Section 2

The Only Rule You'll Ever Need for Eating

The ultimate rule for how to eat and be thin is:
Eat whatever you want
whenever you want
and enjoy it.

Yes. You read that correctly. Eat whatever you want. Likely, no woman has ever been told those words, unless it was a new mother getting instructions from her ob-gyn because she was having trouble lactating. From now on, no food is off-limits. Ever. This may be the most counter intuitive thing you learn here and, consequently, the most effective.

How have you learned to view food? Good. Bad. Right. Wrong. Healthy. Unhealthy. Fattening. Slimming. Forbidden. Allowed. The saying that you always want what you can't have is true and rises to a level of obsession when regarding food. This is what causes a lot of big, fat trouble.

Consider this scenario: There are cookies in the kitchen. Your favorite kind. For me, this would be chocolate chunk cookies. Maybe you bought them for your kids as a treat. Maybe your roommate baked them, or skinny ass Sally from the neighborhood association asked you to take them home after the quarterly meeting so she wouldn't eat them—whatever. They're there. And you really want one. But no! Cookies are bad! Bad, evil, off-limits. You cannot eat them because you are an out-of-control fatso and you must restrict. Must. Resist. (Yummy.) Cookies.

Doesn't this sound like what you are taught, especially when you are dieting? What happens then? You eat an apple to satisfy your sweet tooth. Still obsessing about the cookie, you have a banana too. A few handfuls of fat-free crackers are shoveled into your mouth next. That should satisfy the crave to crunch, right? Nope. A couple spoonfuls of last night's dinner leftovers, cold out of the fridge, seem like they will do the trick. Finally, you chomp down a "healthy" granola bar. You know the kind. The dark chocolate one with almonds you keep as "good" dessert option. But it's puny, bland and really doesn't taste like a cookie. Feeling too far down the hole at this point, you give in and exclaim, "To heck with it!" and eat the cookie. Guilt and shame creep up, so you throw in another cookie or two, to ease the mental anguish you've put yourself through.

I have done this exact thing a thousand times. Always, I wound up hating myself for being so weak, despite best efforts, to resist the wicked cookie. Or pizza. Or fries. Or whatever I'd villainized as my food arch nemesis. Moreover, I was putting down way more calories eating "good" foods, trying to thwart the cookie craving, than if I'd just let myself eat the darn thing.

Let's pause here. To be clear, there are no counting calories in this weight loss method; but, for the sake of quantifying the danger, a cookie is about 200 calories, while an apple (100), banana (100), crackers (120), leftovers (150), granola bar (160)...you get the idea. Calorically, it's way more damaging than just eating the innocent cookie. Also, I was eating way more cookies than I even wanted because I felt frantic about getting as much in as I could before another inevitable round of self-served starvation commenced.

What's for Dinner? Anything

It doesn't have to be this way anymore. You are indeed allowed to eat cookies and anything else you want. Imagine this second scenario: There are cookies in the kitchen and, why, yes, you do want some. You put one (or two) on a plate, pour yourself some coffee, fold a napkin and sit down to enjoy cookies. Mmmm. End of story.

Enjoying that treat was a much easier and leaner option. You have saved yourself a bunch of food in your belly you didn't actually want, a lot of energy-sucking obsession, and—oh yeah—you enjoyed yourself some cookies. But wait! There's more. You may even be amazed to find you don't have an appetite for a while. In fact, you end up eating less at your next meal or over the course of the day because you were plenty satisfied from this treat.

I know you might be thinking, "Oh my god. Ohmygodohmygodohmygod. Maybe some people can do this, but I can't just let myself eat whatever I want. I will go completely out of control and eat until I'm a blimp." Believe me, I carried the same fear for years. You already know what that got me. Fat! I am no one special and I don't have super powers. This way really works. It is not the foods out there that made me gain weight. It was the response to disallowing foods. Letting myself eat whatever I wanted worked to get it off.

Somehow when food is deemed okay to eat, it becomes less desirable or easier to say no to. We say no to so many other things that we enjoy, without any of the struggle. You could stay up another three hours at night to watch a few more episodes of your favorite show, but you know how yucky it feels to be so tired the next day. You stop and go to bed. It's not a problem for you. You're a grown-up with a choice. Again, you could choose to buy that pair of glitter-encrusted, platform heels, but you decide it's better for you to save your money. At home, you've been slaying the day with yard work, pulling weeds, mowing and mulching. You could press on and tackle those overgrown shrubs, but you'd rather save yourself the potential backache that comes with pushing too hard, so you decide to stop. You don't get crushed with the pining of more TV, shopping or extra yard work. You know you can do or have those things at any time, but you choose not to in the present. You've lived and learned. It's the same with food. Live in the present and learn what you really do or do not want.

You may have no problem stopping other activities but feel out of control with food. The change won't happen overnight. It's likely taken years to get to this way of thinking, so be patient as you change. Practice this mental exercise. If you feel yourself panicking when confronted with a "forbidden" food, pause. Take a breath. Consciously tell yourself you can totally eat it if you want to. I still do this for myself. Like, let's say I'm in an airport on a layover and hankering for a snack. Inside the nearest newsstand, I am confronted with walls of candy and chips and delightful, formerly forbidden foods. Even after years of allowing myself to eat anything, I still can get triggered by this and start worrying that something bad would happen if I were to eat whatever was inside one of those enticing cellophane packets. First, I pause to notice my thinking is going down that path. I take a breath and remind myself that I am absolutely allowed to eat whatever I want. Maybe I do want a pack of candy after all or maybe I want some nuts. Either way, it's going to cost me twenty-eight dollars. So I should at least do myself the service of enjoying whichever pricey snack my body truly needs.

Give Your Body Some Cred

Your body knows so much more than you think it does. Trust it in this process. Our bodies are brilliant masters at keeping us alive and well, despite how badly we trash or take them for granted. Think of when you get sick and your immune system signals for immediate attack on invading culprits. Your body wants what is best for you to be a high-functioning, happy, healthy human being. If it needs you to do something to assist in this, it will let you know. When it needs to sleep, you feel tired and you naturally wake up when it's rested. When it is thirsty, you know it automatically and you can sense when you're quenched. Your body tells you when to go to the bathroom and when it is relieved. It even sends signals like when it's ready to make a baby, when it's time to give birth and when it's time to stop making babies. Yay menopause! You trust these messages from your body without question, but have lost trust in your hunger and fullness signals. The head has gotten in the way.

Just like with everything else, your body will tell you what and when to eat. Let it do what it knows to do. It is your thoughts and beliefs that sabotage this natural course, not your body. You want to gradually diminish the power of the thoughts and rules in your mind about food and hunger, and learn to listen and trust the signals in your body. You do this by making all foods allowed.

Let your body take over the decisions of what it wants and needs. Relax. Your body is not going to signal for you to eat all of the french fries in town at once. Eating whatever you want is essentially eating whatever your body wants, not your head.

What your body says it wants to eat may seem unconventional in your head. Gradually, you will learn that this is perfectly fine. Acknowledge those true cravings. Do what your body says. For example, I might have graham crackers dipped in peanut butter for lunch one day. Logically, soup and salad seems like a more appropriate meal, but that's what I wanted. If I wake up in the mood for pesto pasta, that's what I'm having or breakfast. If dinner time rolls around and all I'm really hungry for is a bowl of cereal, dinner is served. I often get jokes about how I eat weird stuff. It's not weird, it's simply what I want. Plus, I also get jokes about being a skinny bitch, so I just take any of those jabs as compliments. From now on, eating is, for real, whatever you want, not an external suggestion.

While you are paying so much attention to what your body wants to eat, you will learn to pay attention to how you feel after eating too. Sure, I have let myself have a family-size bag of Skittles for dinner (by myself and not with any family). I was eating what I wanted, but I really felt icky after. Before finding thinner bliss, I would have done that doused in shame, not really able to enjoy it. But now that I have permission to do this. It removes all guilty, hateful, punishing thoughts and makes room for me to find, "That was tasty, but I actually feel kind of gross." You must remove those feelings of guilt to see how you really feel about eating something. Again, believing all food is allowed is your tool.

Later on when I think I want a smorgasborg of sugar for dinner, I have an understanding of how it actually makes me feel and decide, "I don't really want to feel sick afterwards, and would feel better enjoying fajitas for dinner tonight." And that's it! I know I'm totally allowed to eat whatever I want whenever I want and I freely choose the option I know will feel best.

This attention to your body works both ways. It makes clear what you really want and what you don't. Say the office is picking up fried chicken for lunch. Do you want any? You know it's delicious and you are totally allowed to eat it; but, nah, you don't really feel like that. On date night, your server asks if you'd like dessert. You can order some, sure, but dessert would leave you feeling uncomfortably full. You pass. Those pastries look lovely behind the case at the coffee shop, but you just don't *really* want one.

Sometimes you don't want certain foods because you just don't. Sometimes you don't want them because you know you don't want the feeling that comes after it, and you are able to pass without obsessing about it.

You the Foodie

When you are eating whatever you want, what you want makes a difference. When I first started eating like this, of course I wanted only cake and cheeseburgers and basically everything I had told myself was wrong for ten years. So I ate them. Let the record show, I still lost weight.

I'm not recommending you resign yourself to a diet based on corn syrup. There are probably a hundred dietitians and doctors who'd like to smack me for suggesting folks eat *Ben and Jerry's* instead of a more nutritious dinner. It's common sense not to live on sweets. However, I do want you to start exploring what quality, delicious and really good food offers. Expose your body to better things for it to want.

Maybe you are already a connoisseur of gourmet fare. You understand the delicious difference between a frittata made with farm fresh eggs, seasonal vegetables and cracked pepper over one from a box in the freezer aisle. That's excellent. For anyone who could stand to use more experience in the world of food, your education starts now.

It took me some time to gain mine. I was clueless at first. I mean, I had no idea that food could even taste like anything. Growing up, the staple of my mother's cooking was ground beef, bought on sale then stored in the freezer until it was dinner time. She would put a skillet on high heat then plop the frozen cube of meat into the pan where it would sizzle violently as she stabbed away at it with a spatula. Always, it was turned into a pitiful version of spaghetti, chili or tacos. To this day I cannot bring myself to eat a taco. It's no wonder I grew up believing a candy bar was ambrosia. Between my mother's meat dishes and my stepfather's raw foods diet, I only understood food to taste like cardboard and sadness.

I know quite a few folks who grew up with very different experiences. For them, it was never an issue of food not being allowed, but that fast food and delivery pizza were normal dinner options. They learned that that was the good stuff. Wherever you have been in your culinary background, I encourage you to venture out.

It was cooking that taught me the true wonders of well-made food. Cooking at home has kept me much thinner over all of these years, and it's some of the best advice I can pass along. In my early attempts, I got really into Indian cuisine and found it surprisingly easy to make. The array of spices were thrilling for a palate that had only ever known packaged taco seasoning. Curry. Cardamom. Anise. All different and mouth-watering. I had no idea vegetables could taste so gosh darn delicious when sauteed with these fragrant delights. At first, my skills were awkward at best. Clumsily chopping an onion isn't exactly fun. But the joy of eating what I had cooked was totally worth the effort. Besides, I got way better at it and, not to brag, but I'm kind of like a veggie chopping fiend now. I'm like the Hannibal Lecter of produce, meticulously carving away the most edible bits for my dinner. I'm kind of like...creepy, I guess, so I'll stop.

Along with your own cooking adventures, you can absolutely let yourself adore dishes from restaurant kitchens. We are all stupid lucky to have just about any kind of food readily available. Gourmet has become the new norm in the restaurant world. Chefs are both artists and scientists. Explore their creations. Enjoy it with the tools you are learning here. Try restaurants you have never visited. Experience new-to-you dishes and cuisines. Authentic Chinese food, if you haven't had it before, will knock your socks off. It's nothing like the sticky-sweet orange chicken we all know from take-out. Hunt down the best Mediterranean dive in your neck of the woods. Order feature entrees among fine dining fare. Educate yourself on well-made, thoughtfully crafted food.

No longer do you need to look at a menu and seek out what you think is the least fattening. Order what looks like the most delicious. I have put in my time working restaurant jobs, and it's almost like having psychic abilities when I see a table of ladies dining together. I know, before they even know, which salad they are all going to request because it's the thing that appears to be the lightest menu item. Little do they realize the pecans and dried cranberries on that thing are little sugar bombs.

The dressing that comes with it is also hiding a stock of sweetener, and the lean-sounding grilled chicken is doused in oil before thrown on the fire. To top it off, those "healthy" lettuce leaves basically become a backdrop for the cheese pile that's dumped in. I've known places to take yesterday's dinner rolls, quarter and fry them, to make croutons. So four croutons in and you've eaten a bread roll soaked in oil. Not very good if we're going for something lean here. This anomaly for ordering said salad seems to worsen under peer pressure. None of us ladies want to look like the fatty, ordering the fried fish entree, so we order the skinny salad like Patty and Marge did. Just get what you want, girls. Be the brave, independent, less-fat superwoman. Order that barbecue chicken with extra butter on a side of cornbread. Show the other girls how it's done.

Whenever's Clever

We're on a roll here, breaking a bunch of old dieting rules. Here's another one to blow to smithereens: *when* to eat. Eat whenever you want. There is no breakfast time. No lunch time. No snack time. No times are allotted for eating or times you should restrict. Your body is going to let you know when it's eating time.

I went through a number of years where I always got super hungry around four o'clock in the afternoon. But I had it in my little, highlighted blonde head that dinner should be at six. I told the rumbling hunger pangs that they were wrong and to hush, as if I knew better. I was all talk and no game. I ceaselessly reached for little snacks, hastily eaten out of irritation. By the time six o'clock rolled around, I had nibbled enough to constitute a whole meal but without experiencing the satisfaction of sitting down to enjoy one, so I would have a full dinner too. I was eating two dinners worth of food every day, and my waistline showed it.

Then it dawned on me, "Hey, I'm a grown-ass woman. I can eat whenever I want." Hello, light bulb! I started having a big, late afternoon meal when I was hungry. Imagine that. I would be satisfied enough to not want dinner later. Sometimes I did a workout in the evening. Other times, I had a very light, late dinner, like a cup of soup and a glass of wine. When anyone asked me to join them for dinner I would usually pass, joking that I wasn't much of a dinner-eater and suggest something else to do together. I slimmed down quite a bit as a result of this realization.

At the time, I was employed in a remote sales position. The flexible, work-from-home schedule allowed me to accommodate this pattern. Then I was promoted and moved to work out of the headquarters office in a different state. I worked a lot of late hours, and it was no longer feasible to enjoy that four o' clock meal time. Thanks to my prior revelation, I knew better not to get hung up on rules about eating times, even if I was the one who made up the rules. I found the right adjustment for my body. I lightly grazed during the day, usually every few hours. I saved my biggest meal for late in the evening, knowing that was going to be the awesome dinner I could savor. This was quite the reverse of what I used to do, but I stayed trim and carried on because I was not hung up on the rules of specific times to eat

Obviously, we can't all go around intuitively eating whenever we want. Schedules are a necessity for most everything else in life. Look for a balance in your real world schedule and when your body is asking to be fed. If you're ready for dinner as soon as you're home for the day, have it. It's been said breakfast boosts your metabolism, but if you're not hungry in the morning, don't eat. Then if you need lunch at 10:30 AM, cool. If you have regular meal times to accommodate family or work, that's perfectly fine. The goal is for you to understand times to eat are not a universal law. Find what works best for you around your life, not based on someone else's suggested timeline.

Give those old rules about what to eat and when a big, slobbery kiss goodbye!

This is How We Chew It

This is a big one. I hope you're ready. It's a lot to handle, so brace yourself. Here goes.

How to eat is...drum roll please...*enjoy it*.

That's right, ladies and gentlemen. Actually taking pleasure in eating food leads down the path of thinner bliss. This is no snake oil sales pitch. It's for real. Use your goddess-given senses to take in aromas and flavors. Savor each bite so you can appreciate your fare of choice. Slow down. Chew. Allow eating to be an experience of lasting pleasure.

I discovered the happy effects of this by accident, years before any of these methods were on my radar. I was twenty-one, young, dumb and extra chubby. It hadn't dawned on me that slamming half-price whiskey sours all night with my girlfriends would have an effect on my dress size. It sure as shootin' did, in a big way. A twenty extra pounds kind of way. I handled my weight gain with the poise, competence and guile of a thoughtless maniac. Triathlons! Yeah! I signed up for a couple and hastily mapped out a training plan. I was going to get all buff and stuff and look amazing. The old extremist ways for weight loss were still alive and kicking, this time, under the guise of a run, bike, swim race. This latest scheme had nothing to do with actually being strong or feeling fit, even though I pretended it did. It was always about wanting to look hot.

And that's how I wound up spending a summer with my bouncy butt in a swimsuit doing laps, blobbing down running paths and cycling for miles. These were non-competitive events put on by the YMCA, but I carbo-loaded like an ironman champion. True to form, I didn't enjoy a bite and felt frantic about everything I ate. I tried to follow an athlete's prescribed diet, but if there's anyone on Earth who cannot stick to a diet, it's me. Three months of training and two triathlons later (one I almost didn't make it to because I was so hungover), guess how many pounds I lost. Zero! And no, I don't want to hear that excuse about muscle weighing more than fat. I was not muscular and still chunky.

"That does it!" I thought. Clearly I had no idea how to lose weight, and I was ready to write myself off as a lost cause. Totally frustrated I told myself, "If I'm going to be fat, I might as well at least enjoy my food. Ugh!" It was a pouty and defeated resignation. I felt like I was hitting a bottom with myself, so I figured I should at least get something good from my problem.

I did. And, amazingly, lost weight. I knew I was going to eat cheesecake anyway, but instead of shamefully gobbling it down, I took time to really taste it. I sat my butt down at a table and paid attention to the burrito, pasta, bowl of cereal, or whatever, and before I knew it, I had less of a butt.

At the time, I didn't quite make the connection between enjoying food and losing weight. I still needed a few more years of feeding my head case, falling back into drastic dieting and exercising, followed by gorging fit for Roman-era celebrations. When I was ready to change for good, I went back to enjoying food and have never stopped. It's a pleasure savoring the array of rich flavors, textures, temperatures and overall experience of quality food. I will go for one bite of a rich, decadent, real chocolate truffle over a bag of Oreos any day. Try savoring an Oreo. It can't be done. There simply isn't the complexity as that of well-made desserts. Over the years, I have developed tangible, applicable tools to help keep this up and keep me trim. I still use them today and now they are here for you.

This first one you've likely heard before: Put your food down between bites. It is one of the most helpful tactics for me and if you have heard this advice elsewhere, hear it again. I'm not claiming to have invented this tool, but I am here to reiterate it to you and be living proof that it works. Put your fork, spork, fingers or chopsticks down between bites. This practice slows your eating down. Like, way down, giving you ample time to enjoy it. I can eat half of my dinner this way and feel just as full as if I had eaten the whole thing quickly.

In order for this to work, you are going to have to do it perfectly all of the time. Only kidding! I slip up on this plenty and start getting a little belly to show for it. I know to tell myself, "Darling. You need to start putting your food down between bites, mkay?" It's my first line of defense against fatness. Sometimes you might forget too or simply be in a rush. Do your best. Maybe you work somewhere that only allows thirty minutes for a lunch break, not nearly enough to slowly chew every morsel. That's fine. Let your lunch serve the utilitarian purpose of fueling you for the work day, and save the savoring for when you're home.

A common protest to this tactic is, "I don't have time. I'm always in a rush and have to eat whatever quickly." I get it. I really do. But you love yourself now. Remember how we went over that? So how about being a doll and bumping up "extra time to eat" on your priority list? Is it more inconvenient for you than dealing with extra body weight?

Having children can certainly pose a challenge to the time factor. Children are precious, fulfilling and also, well, rather time-consuming. I completely understand that, for a parent, being asked to eek out one more minute in the day may feel like too much. However, part of me will always wish I had parents model behaviors for enjoying my food and taking my time with it. It would have saved a lot of grief and struggle. I hope more of us will learn to do this for the benefit of the kiddos today.

On some occasions, it's simply the sensation of scarfing down a bucket of movie popcorn, not even a millisecond between bites, that hits the spot. I know I definitely have these urges, except it's with candy. Let yourself have those treats, but just keep on eye on it so it doesn't become a thoughtless habit. For the rest of the time, this tool is one to keep at the ready. When life is getting hectic and you are rushing through meals, follow this step and hit the reset button. It is the loveliest feeling knowing you can have anything you want to eat; you get to enjoy it, and you get to weigh your perfect weight.

Another trick I use is portioning out my food. I don't mean three ounces of fish, five ounces of vegetables, half a cup of rice, blah blah blah don't make me gag. Do not use measuring implements to serve yourself food. I mean take the amount of food you want to eat, the portion you determine, and separate it from the original container. To put it plainly, don't eat chips out of the bag. I eat chips and crackers and tasty snacky stuff all the time. The difference is, I take what I want from the bag, put it in a little dish and sit myself down to savor it. As a result, I have no issues with potato chips, I like liking them and don't put on weight. I'm telling you this works. Also, don't look at nutrition labels. I staunchly avoid these. Who is Nabisco to tell me that a serving size is seventeen crackers or whatever? A serving size is what I feel like eating at the time.

While you're putting food onto another dish, make it a nice dish. Don't just dump it onto a paper towel and hold it in your hand. You deserve better than that, my sweet. Presentation is a useful tool too. We all know how nice it is when we eat out, because someone else has done the cooking and the serving for us. I think another, often overlooked, bonus of restaurant dining is having a proper place setting. Give yourself that luxury at home too. From a snack to a three-course meal, use nice dishes, napkins and appropriate utensils. Having a beautiful place setting adds to the enjoyment of your food which, as we now know, is a key to losing weight. So start getting all Susie Homemaker with your table.

I've developed a fetish for cloth napkins and place mats. Even when I have a little snack, I have a set of cute, miniature bowls to use. One day, all of my snack bowls were in the dishwasher when I wandered in the kitchen for some yogurt. In a bind, I put the yogurt in a martini glass with a dollop of whipped cream, and the presentation made that yogurt snack the best to date!

You can make your table fancy as fudge, with your crystal glasses, china, and Martha Stewart-worthy centerpiece, but there is one thing you may not have: Distractions. No cell phone, no TV, no radio, no reading material. Did I mention cell phones? I know we are all so enamored with our phones. How could we not be? Phone world is way more enticing than the real world with its chores, debt and mirrors that show our faces without digital touch-ups. Every time I slip and keep my phone at the table, I soon find a dirty, empty plate in front of me and am like, "Wait. What? Did I even eat anything?" It's a sure fire way to wind up overeating because I'm not noticing fullness or I don't have a sense of satisfaction from enjoying a meal. I need to leave my phone in a faraway room to avoid this. If it's anywhere near me, there's this sense like I have an infant with the flu that needs constant checking-on. (Do I have a phone addiction?)

Let's all remember to eat and not multi-task. I think if more people paid half as much attention to enjoying food as they do their phones, weight would be less of a problem. Another tidbit for avoiding distraction is to sit down while you eat too. When I eat standing up, it feels like I might need to rush off at a moment's notice. Sitting down is relaxing.

There's one more thing to keep in mind while you are putting all of this into practice. You don't have to eat everything on your plate. When you are sitting down and eating your food slowly, you are sure to find yourself full before you get to the end of what you've served. That is completely fine. It's good! Being able to turn away food because you are full is the way to weight loss. I don't push the best-looking bites around my plate, saving them in a corner to eat last, after eating all the rest. I dive right in and get the good bites up front. That's what you want to fill up on. This is a very effective way to feel full from a good meal without even finishing the whole thing, which in turn trims a body down.

There is some deep-seated guilt in those of us who were taught to eat our whole dinner because: 1) we couldn't leave the table until we did, or 2) we would be withheld dessert, or 3) we were made to feel guilty because there were starving children somewhere else in the world. Don't feel badly. I do way worse than that. Sometimes I will throw almost all of my food away. For example, if someone brings donuts to the office, I'm torn because they look delicious, but I know I will feel pretty gross if I eat a whole donut. So I literally will take one bite of the donut and throw the rest away. If you really want to help starving children, there are charities for that. The extra food on your plate isn't going to help them whether it goes in your belly or in the trash. So, instead, feel good if you are satiated before your food is gone, and bask in its slenderizing effects.

Bottoms Up

Add a drink to your repertoire of weight loss tips. I put drinks into three categories: heavy, lean and water. Water will get a closer look in the last section. The only point I want to add about it here is I do not recommend plain water with food. It seems to make the flavors more bland. Find a complementary beverage instead. Lean drinks include, but are not limited to: soda water, tea and coffee. Basically drinks that do not wash down a bunch of calories. Heavy drinks would be booze, juices, soda and all sorts of sweetened elixirs.

Drinks are a wonderful way to round out the whole eating experience. Wine pairs beautifully with specific foods, while other food items, like a cheeseburger, just beg to be with a soda. Enhancing your experience with a drink, in turn, adds to your total satisfaction, which is the key to being slender. On the flip side, beverages can be an all-too-easy way to put more in your body than it needs, leading to weight gain. This is especially true with soda. It's too much like liquid sugar and, when imbibed thoughtlessly, it has the same effect.

Years back I was being treated by a chiropractor. (I was hit by a car on my bicycle. True story.) When I first started to see him, he was the tall, brawny type. Then, one day, I showed up for an appointment and he was suddenly the tall, lanky type. I was like, "Dr. Chiropractor, where did half of you go?" He told me he had given up sugary sodas and lost thirty pounds. Thirty pounds! Just for quitting soda.

If you drink a lot of sweet soda and want to cut it out entirely, like Dr. Chiropractor did, that's a great decision. It's one you get to make, and I certainly won't stand in your way. My advice for heavy drinks is simply to learn to enjoy them just like you do with food. Sip your wine, margarita or orange cream soda slowly. Put it in a beautiful glass or an expensive glass or a rad, retro drinking glass, with Smurf characters on it that you found at the flea market. Pay attention to its quality, flavors, temperature, bubbliness and how it makes you feel. Thoughtlessly drinking heavy beverages while you are doing other things adds up much too quickly. Just like you learn to not eat chips out of a bag while standing up and scrolling through your phone, you don't want to chug Cherry Cola while driving around running errands. Save it for when you can savor it.

Also like food, drink what you want. Say you're gracing a swanky little bistro and thinking, "I could so go for a martini, but it has too many calories. I'll just have a light beer." Stop right there! You go for that martini, you sassy little socialite, with its oh-so-salty olives, brandished by a dainty skewer. Savor it. Indulge in it. Let it satisfy you infinitely more than a few bottles of beer-flavored water.

I find a lot of the lean drink options can hit the spot just as much as or more than heavy ones. Soda water is one of my faves. Nothing quite compares to a cold can, cracked fresh from the fridge, itty bitty bubbles dancing under my nose as I go for that first sip that's so refreshing, it hurts my face.

Twelve-packs of soda water are a supermarket staple these days with flavor options galore. When I first began my path to thinner bliss, this just wasn't a thing. The best I could do was buy liter bottles of Perrier, which were expensive and always went flat before I could finish a bottle. Now entire aisles are dedicated to sparkling water. Tea is another go-to, especially for pairing with food.

I'm a southern lady. It's common practice, where I come from, to specify if you'd like sweet or unsweet tea, when ordering in a restaurant. Yes, that's a real thing. Sweet tea technically qualifies as a heavy drink as it's soaking in sugar. Again, it's not a problem as long you're not swigging it thoughtlessly. Unsweetened tea, especially hot tea, is something I've been getting geeky over. It comes in a zillion flavor combinations, from enticing salted caramel to weird ginger rhubarb. In addition, I'm a self-proclaimed coffee addict. My gateway cup was a can of double espresso from a gas station refrigerator, loaded with cream and sugar. Gradually, I have removed the additives from my cup of joe and revel in a piping hot, pour of caffeinated bliss, taken black.

Whatever your drink of choice, take it with the time and pleasure you are having with food. To that I say, "Cheers to you, darling!"

Summary of Tools

- Eat whatever you want.
- Trust your body.
- Pay attention to what your body wants and doesn't want.
- Experience well-made, high quality, really good food.

- Cook for yourself.
- Enjoy your food.
- Put your food down between bites.
- Remove your desired portion of food from the original container.
- Serve your food with a nice presentation.
- Do not have distractions while you are eating.
- You do not need to finish everything on your plate.
- Enjoy drinks just like you enjoy your food.

Section 3

Weight-Life Balance

The number one, sure-fire way I have found to gain weight is deprivation. Deprivation was a self-inflicted torment I endured to lose weight in the past. It led to hunger, irritability, exhaustion, and, eventually–always– gaining weight again. For lifelong weight loss, I have found balance instead.

Balance helps prevent deprivation and manage sensations of hunger. It also considers making adjustments for life changes. As always, there are some cool tools to help you do this. These include: offsetting, making little cuts and substitutions. All of that without losing your mind. Balance is the Elmer's school glue in those macaroni noodle crafts we used to do. You remember the ones, with the cotton balls and googly eyes and copious amounts of glitter. Consider everything you've learned up to this point as the macaroni and stuff that need to be put together and arranged into masterful, weight loss, noodle art.

Delete Deprivation

Deprivation is, by definition, the denial of a necessity. In this case, food. You intentionally keep yourself from food and experience a strong sense of lack. If you are familiar with the horrors of dieting, you are well-acquainted with what deprivation feels like. It sucks. Since diets are usually propelled by feeling badly about your body, it makes it even extra sucky. Deprivation leads to obsession which leads to overeating and fatness.

Think about a day when you have had a lack of sleep. Your tiredness overpowers your ability to function in almost every way. Getting more sleep is all you can think about. It consumes you. It's called sleep deprivation for a reason, and it's a problem. A lack of sleep impedes your happiness and productive functioning. It's an inefficient way to subsist, and that anyone would intentionally inflict this same torment with food, in the name of losing weight, is no good either.

Unless, heaven forbid, the world experiences famine, deprivation only comes from within. In other words, purposefully restricting yourself from food. However, choosing not to have something because you truly feel you will be fine without it, and you want to take care of your body, is balance. Understanding the difference takes practice. Be patient and gentle. Allowing all foods and enjoying them is the basis for preventing deprivation and discovering choice. This is a sense you will develop on your own, like a super cool sixth sense, as you continue living by these methods. Find your balance between reveling in the right foods your body chooses and removing the excess. It's your guide to get thin and stay that way.

Hello, Hunger

Coming from a background of food restriction, I struggled with handling hunger for a long time. It wasn't until maybe the past year that I finally made peace with it. Hopefully you will get there sooner than I did. I can surely thank years of anorexia where I taught myself that hunger equaled suffering and needed to be tolerated, as much and as long as possible. Still, years into living with these methods, I would mentally agonize if the slightest pangs of hunger occurred. It was like my brain was dialing 911 and calling for an ambulance to rush over—with snacks.

While I, of course, enjoyed those snacks, it often left me with little appetite for full meals. I wound up doing the grazing thing a lot. This way of eating isn't a problem, but my fear of hunger was. I was not always in a position to grab a bite and could be entirely distracted by the affliction of feeling hungry. I needed to make peace with it, so it didn't disrupt my life by taking all of my attention with fear.

My problem was that I was resisting hunger, much like I had resisted certain foods. In the same way, it led to obsession. I learned to let hunger be as allowable as any other sensation of my body. Hunger happens. Multiple times a day. Accept it.

I also have a totally adorbs boyfriend to thank, who really helped me change my outlook on hunger. He came from a pretty normal eating background. He had been allowed whatever junk food kids like and had a good relationship with food. Wildly different from my childhood, where I was told that Fruit Roll-Ups were toxic. As an adult, he discovered quality, delicious, well-made food on his own and knows how to enjoy an excellent meal. Let it be also known the man has always been lean and never struggled with weight. Kind of crazy how that works, right?

In sharing meals together, he soon noticed my habit of reaching for a snack, often right before we were about to eat. It would leave me "not that hungry" for the nice dinner we ordered at a restaurant, or something we had both put good work into making.

He started encouraging me when I was inclined to snack. "Wait," he said, "Don't ruin your appetite. Wait, so you enjoy your meal."

I told him that I didn't want to be hungry. He shared that his response to hunger was excitement. It made him look forward to eating something amazing for, obviously, hunger means it's time to eat! My subconscious response to hunger had been, "This is a sign of torment, I must eradicate it at once!" His response was, "Yay! It's time to enjoy something delicious. I am looking forward to it and can totally live with the sensation of hunger until then." It's normal to feel hungry leading up to a meal. He has always understood that. I agonized. He anticipated. I learned to anticipate too.

Handling hunger takes balance. I still can get to a point of such hunger that when I do eat, I struggle to slow down and enjoy it because my hunger has gotten out of hand. Plus, many of us know the evils of hangriness. I can go full blown Jekyll 'n Hyde if I'm not careful. I am learning to find how much of a sensation of hunger I can be comfortable with, as I know something good to eat is coming, and at what point I really do need to curb it.

Live in Harmony

By now, you know I have no qualms about allowing myself to enjoy treats. A super duper handy tool that helps me do this is one I call offsetting. Have your cake and offset it later. This particular cake, let's say, is birthday cake someone brought to the office for middle manager Ned. You get yourself a nice slice of that sweet rectangle, after a boisterous, off-key round of "Happy Birthday." You even scored yourself a corner piece with extra frosting.

(You people who say you don't like frosting, I don't understand you. You know who you are.) Have that cake, Marie Antoinette style. Then, to offset it, add ten minutes of cardio to your workouts for the next couple of days. Switch your evening glass of wine for herbal tea. Have carrots instead of crackers for a snack—or any combination of the above.

When I'm satisfied from enjoying something awesome earlier, I don't suffer from cutting a bit here and a bit there. This is an extension of the benefits from savoring the treat. I feel so content from that experience that making up for it a bit comes nowhere near feeling like I'm restricting. I am happy to do it. This does not have to be a source of strife. Remember how it's no problem to choose to not make a frivolous purchase, because it's better for you to save your money. You make these choices from loving yourself and taking care of magnificent you!

Finding balance with this tool has been a total one-eighty opposite of how I once behaved. In my dark ages of dieting, I thought any pleasures had to be earned by way of some preceding suffering. Like, as soon as I get to a size two then I will be allowed to eat again. When I can slip into a teeny bikini then I can hang out at the pool. Once I lose five pounds then I can dunk my face in a bag of M&M'S. Maybe this approach came from parents saying, "Eat your vegetables then you can have dessert." While there is obviously merit to this instruction, all I heard was the yummy stuff must be earned by torture.

To an eight-year-old, eating vegetables was just that.

Apply this tool to different scenarios, like a Swiss Army Knife of weight loss survival. It's not just for having a pastry. If I join friends for a big, greasy brunch, I lighten up the rest of the day. Sometimes I will have a whole day or a few days that are just filled with eating, like the holidays. I will choose to offset that for a few days afterwards. Even within the course of a meal, this tool is usable. For instance, if I go for an appetizer when out to dinner, I'll pass on a cocktail and dessert.

While the formula is usually to eat first offset later, once in a while it works the opposite direction. If I'm planning to visit grandma, whose love language is a continuous onslaught of home baked goods, I may keep things light in advance. Sometimes I won't and just make up for it after, or sometimes it's a little bit of both. As long as you are enjoying your food, the offsetting comes easily. That's balance, my friends. You get to feel out an equilibrium that works for you.

I make little cuts in my eating, even when I'm not offsetting something. Nixing a bit here and there adds up over time. If you think about it, a diet requires cutting a lot of food out to generate rapid weight loss. If you were to take the equivalent of all those diet cuts and stretch them out over a much longer time, you could still end up losing the same amount of weight and with the added mega bonus of keeping it off.

I go about this by asking myself the question: Can I live without it?

Can I live without putting cheese on my sandwich? Yes. Can I live without the chips and queso appetizer? Yes. Can I live without the blob of whipped cream I like on my afternoon coffee? No. Can I live without croutons on my salad? Yes. Can I live without popcorn during the movie? No. Can I live without a beer from the fridge? Yes.

While it is important to cut out or exchange foods to lose weight, it is equally as important to do so only to a point that you don't feel a similar sense of lack any diet could conjure. Remember you are going for balance here. You learn to determine what is just the right amount of food to satisfy you, without cutting too much to where you feel deprived. It's like deciding what to wear if you're a Vegas stripper. It should be little enough to get the job done, but enough to keep it legal. As you gradually get comfortable with all food being allowed, it will be easier to let go of little pieces. It becomes a back and forth motion of what to nix and what to keep like a dance, and one you can do with a strong sense of balance. Like those same strippers learn to dance in those mile-high heels. Ain't no shame! A girls gotta maker her money. (And those ladies probably make a lot more than some of us.)

Another extra sexy thing you can use is this tried-and-true weight loss tool I use on almost a daily basis. Substitution. Swap out certain foods for leaner options. Instead of making a sandwich on bread, turn it into a wrap. Vegetable noodles are an amazing sub for carbs in a number of entrees. Butternut squash noodles, found in the freezer section, are my favorite for cooking pad thai. In the morning, instead of eggs and toast, perhaps eggs and fruit will do just fine. I can sweeten my bowl of breakfast oats with applesauce instead of the cascade of honey I usually go for. Instead of two pieces of pizza, I can opt for one and add a salad. If I'm getting the munchies (and not because I smoke, because I don't), sometimes just a stick of gum is enough. A glass of soda water would be plenty perfect with dinner as wine, and I still pour it in a wine glass to be fancy.

Make substitutions for yourself. Pay attention to what is truly sufficient to properly feed your splendid body, and what will leave you wanting more. There will certainly be times where you could easily cut or sub something, but you just know that, if you do, you will wind up feeling deprived. Some good old-fashioned trial and error has also taught me my limitations. Pretend I get through all of my meals for the day. I swapped and reduced carbs like a pro, but before bedtime I am feeling a bit of an itch. Half a bag of chips and a few beers later, it's alleviated. Guess I wasn't as satisfied as I thought.

This way of living is meant to be successfully used the

rest of your life. Life—it's gonna change. The methods I have found are flexible enough to change alongside it. Weight loss plans that require certain times, specific foods and amounts get thrown out the window as soon there are dining out plans, a trip or any unexpected obligation. None of those will interfere with this new lifestyle. It's an internal method rather than external rules, applicable to life changes.

A lot of times when a scheduling disruption occurs in a person's life, I notice him or her saying that once the transition is over then they will get back to "being good." That, "as soon as the stress of my daughter's move to college is over then I will go back to the gym." Or, "as soon as we get back from Europe then I will get back on my diet." Or even, "as soon as the holidays are over then I'm going to hit the treadmill hard." I, too, thought this way and existed on the strictest schedule to eat and exercise. If anything occurred beyond my rule book, I couldn't handle the change and usually fell completely off the wagon, swearing I would get back to living on 800 calories a day, as soon as everything around me evened out.

Nowadays, that anything, from an impromptu lunch date or new career, makes no difference in my understanding of how to take care of my body feels remarkable. Once, thanks to a whopping round of lay-offs, I wound up working back in restaurants for a while. Shifts varied wildly and I would regularly work twelve hours or more without a chance to eat. This was quite the change to the eating schedule I was accustomed to. But, luckily, I had already figured out all of this thinner bliss stuff. I listened to my body, adjusted accordingly and managed to stay perfectly thin and feel fine.

In a decade of life changes, I have moved from having small meals about six times a day to having my biggest meal in the morning and tapering off my intake into the evening, to one large main meal of the day at some unconventional time. These days, for whatever reason, I eat three sturdy meals and never snack.

Not one of these patterns has been bad or better than another. Throughout them all, I have loved my body, loved food and used my tools of offsetting, little cuts, substitution, managing hunger and avoiding deprivation. It has allowed me to live a dynamic life, free from worry to enjoy what I eat and when.

Summary of Tools

- Accept your hunger as a natural signal to enjoy eating.
- Manage your hunger so it does not overtake your eating.

- Offset the indulgences you eat with small food and beverage cuts and additional exercise.
- Make small, manageable cuts in your food and drink intake, as you go along the day.
- Ask yourself, "Can I live without it?"
- Substitute food and drinks with leaner options, where plausible.
- Avoid deprivation.

Section 4

Exercise and Other Good-for-You Stuff

To lose weight and keep it off, we need to exercise. Bet you've never heard that one before. Oh, you have? Like a zillion times? Ah, well, as you know then, exercise is so dang good for you that it is worth saying again. While you could surely follow all of the eating guidelines in this book, never workout, and still lose weight, I would be doing a disservice by not including this as a part of thinner bliss living. It is a regular part of my life that has been essential for keeping me trim.

As with eating, there is no exercise plan or schedule that is right or wrong. The best I can do is explain how I have approached exercise and how the principles we've learned, up to this point, apply here too. My core concept for exercise is whatever makes my body feel fit and challenged. If I feel like I'm all ready to get decked out and sexy, I know my exercise is sufficient.

As with food, I once had a very unhealthy relationship with exercise. Back when I was hopelessly devoted to anorexia, I was also averaging a ludicrous four hours a day at the gym. (Kids, don't try this at home.) I hated every minute of it. That's, like, 240 minutes to hate. Every day. And to think how short life can be.

Long after I conquered the eating disorder, it was still stuck in my head that for exercise to be effective it had to be extreme. (Recall the triathlons.) I inadvertently proved myself wrong when I figured out thinner bliss. The only exercise I did when I started this journey was— get this—walk. That's all. Let it be known, it was a lot of walking. I lived in Chicago without a car, and worked fourteen-hour shifts on my feet; so, it was perhaps a tad above average. I'm not a numbers girl but, if you must know, a day like that could amount to at least 20,000 steps.

Without considering the amount of walking I did, the activity reaped a benefit beyond losing weight. I learned I did not have to disrupt my world or give up my life to get a workout. It was part of it, in sync with my lifestyle. Also, it wasn't torture. That's not to say workouts will always, seamlessly and easily fall in line with the rest of your schedule. Time to exercise needs to be carved out. It's a priority worth making.

Fitness for (Real) Life

The approach to exercise does differ from the approach to eating, a bit. With eating, we don't count calories or points or grams or carbs. With exercise, without counting reps or minutes or miles or speed, we wouldn't make very much progress. Since we are lucky enough to live in a day and age where we no longer must jump across boulders to escape a bear, or chase down a beaver for dinner, we need a way to gauge if we are getting enough activity. Use tools for measuring exercise to account for this. You know when you are pushing your body and when you could do more. Adapt these measurements to your understanding of what makes your body feel fit and challenged.

Personally, the one line I draw with measuring physical activity is with wearables. As much as I'm sure FitBit wants to write me a big sponsorship check to promote their product, I'm just not a fan. Much of what I understand about maintaining weight is based on my own sense of what I need and how things feel. I wince at the idea of a little machine attached to me, counting steps or measuring sleep patterns, respiration, farts or whatever else it does. All of my natural, physical processes are perfectly fine, thank you very much. If something is out of whack, my body will let me know. I don't need a digital watch to do that work for me. However, that is me. If a wearable works for you then wear it with pride!

Changing up my workout routines and activities has made exercise sustainable for the long run. In the early days of being thinner bliss, the idea of doing anything other than endless cardio and painful calisthenics was really scary, because of how ingrained it was in my dense, little head that that was the way to go. I was sure anything else wouldn't be enough to burn fat, and I would get heavy again. Alternatively, I wasn't willing to give up all of my free time to the treadmill anymore. If my fear proved to be true, I would either have to accept it or be open to the possibilities of other kinds of working out.

I recalled a roommate, from a few years prior, who had a rockin' bod. I asked her what she did to be so fit as a fiddle, and was shocked when she said she lifted weights. No cardio, only weights. I had always thought weight lifting was reserved for beefy men wanting to be beefier, or women who were already trim and wanting to tone. I didn't believe I fit into either category, especially that of the women. But I gave it a whirl. I trekked to a nearby YMCA on the reg and started a routine. The results were astonishing. Not only did I get in shape, I started to cross over into the gratifying realm of thin.

Now, hold up. Don't everybody go run out and start lifting weights just because that's what I did. It's not the specific activity I'm advocating, but the mindset. I allowed other workouts to be an option and let go of the ridiculous form of exercise I used to do. Also, let's have ourselves a look at those insidious little words "used to." Often, when I hear people talk about their weight problems, I hear a lot of those words. "I used to run five miles a day." "I used to workout with a trainer every morning." "I used to do P90X." (Actually, that last one, I have to give that person props. Have you ever done P90X? Oh my god. So hard.) What I'm really hearing, though, is, "As soon as I get back to that workout/habit/level of fitness, everything will be okay. I won't have weight problems."

That is no different than recalling some diet you "used to" stick to. You are not living in the past. Just as you have learned to love your body as it is now and enjoy your food now, you will exercise for the now too. Free yourself from the resistance bands tying you to your workouts past. Tell yourself, "Great job, sweet pea!" and let your adorable heart swell with pride over that physical goal you once conquered. Then move on. Do not measure yourself today by the workout you used to do yesterday, or yesteryear, or yester-back-in-your-twenties.

There's likely a good reason you don't do that workout anymore. I think a lot of people simply burn out. I know I have. I am guilty of pushing myself so hard and so far with a regimen that when it's completed, either by achieving a goal or burn out, I am so exhausted I go way too long getting no exercise at all. It's a lot like a diet. The draconian inhumanity required to get through it is so severe, I never want to pay attention to my eating or lift a dumbbell again.

Even if you don't burn out, life adjustments crop up that can make your current workout plan too inconvenient to continue. For example, my weight lifting worked wonders for me until I moved to a different town. The only nearby gym was hella expensive, and I was short on cash. I also didn't have as much time in my schedule and, let me tell you, weight lifting routines can fill up a girl's dance card right quick. So, I looked for something to fit my current situation. Something that would still make me feel fit and challenged. I discovered high intensity interval training I could do from home and quickly. Again, the change of activity rendered fabulous results.

I kept that up for a while; then after another move, I got into running. With a job change, dance classes. Later on, it was home workout videos, yoga and even hula hooping. Recall how the previous section discussed having flexibility to change your eating patterns and schedules to move with life, while sticking to your core principles. Apply that to your workout too. Don't let yourself completely go just because life shifts. Hang on to the commitment to move in a way that keeps you feeling fit and challenged and adjust accordingly.

Even without some major transition, I still go through phases of exercise. In addition to other activities I've mentioned, I've had a rollerblading phase, an ultimate Frisbee phase, a kickboxing phase, a Pilates phase, and even what I call my StairMaster phase. They have all been a blast. It's a thrill to see what this somewhat wimpy body is capable of. If I had been hung up on wishing I could get back to something I used to do, no one would have had the supreme joy of witnessing this white girl try to waggle her way through a hip hop class. These phases have lasted from a few months to a few years. By paying attention to my body, I can feel when it's simply time to mix it up and when I'm pushing myself to a point of no return. I've gotten to a place where I feel excited to find a new exercise to get into.

Just as you've learned to enjoy food, it would be ideal to enjoy exercise too. But let's be real. Sometimes working out just plain sucks. Even for me, many times the hardest part of my day is getting myself to go workout. That includes days I have to call my mother. (Just kidding. You know I love you, Mom.) Luckily, I've found a magic formula that makes all of the workout misery vanish. Oh, wait. Er, nope. Never mind. I haven't actually. It would have been cool though if I had. The best I can tell you is that I tell myself, "Don't think, just do."

Dwelling on how much I don't want to workout makes the task even harder, so telling myself not to think about it helps move my butt a smidge. Always, always, always I feel better about exercising and am glad I did. Remember how you made choices about what you do or do not eat, just like you make choices to go to bed earlier, or to pay a bill instead of buy shoes. Exercise is the same choice. You are a grown-ass adult who can choose to do the thing that is best for you, even if it's not your most immediate desire.

Goals help me get motivated too. Fitness goals are a normal and good thing to have. There are general fitness goals worth setting like being able to do twenty push-ups, the splits, or run a fast mile. For me, someday I'm going to be able to do one whole pull-up. There are goals that involve wanting to look your best. For example, you may be planning a beach vacation. You want to slay an outfit at a music festival this summer. Maybe, you know you're going to see your ex at your friend's upcoming wedding, and you want to be sure he regrets losing you for the rest of his life. Whatever reason works for you is a good reason.

I once thought I needed to look like a swimsuit model, photoshoot ready all the time, every day. Wouldn't that be a dream? Thank goodness I came to my senses and realized it's great to look and be in good enough shape, and that if I have a reason to amp up my fitness—set a goal. Therefore, I teeter between sustainable activity to a hyped-up challenge and back. I'm constantly in motion, and this is so much better than the all-or-nothing raging bull or sleepy sloth pattern.

On the note of consistent activity, here are a few other tips I wish to impart. In your eating, you find small cuts add up. In your activity, small additions do too. I am one to park at the back of parking lots for extra walking. (Plus there are always plenty of spaces back there, and I don't have to circle around endlessly in search of one by the door.) I take the stairs instead of the elevator, escalator or those moving sidewalks at airports. Actually, the moving sidewalks I usually do take. I tend to be forever dashing to some soon-to-depart plane, needing every iota of extra momentum I can get. But you know what I mean. Also, instead of driving from one place to the next in shopping centers, I walk to each stop. Even at home, I'm happy to make extra trips up and down stairs to fetch laundry and put things away. This all adds to keeping me on the thin side.

It's a balance, just like all parts of thinner bliss are. You want to be pushing yourself physically enough that you get positive changes. Alternatively, learn to feel when you are asking too much of your body. I love the glowy after-burn of a good, hard workout. Yet sometimes, I have to scale back on how hard I push because I've learned to sense when I'm verging on a burn-out. I want to consistently be able to exercise over a long, long time, and avoid overdoing it. It's a sense no one can teach you. It must be practiced. Learned.

Here's one last, nifty trick with exercise. There can be times when I am not paying attention to my eating, I'm not liking my body so much and my gym bag is...heck, I don't even know where it is. I'm in a rut and I just can't seem to get out of my head to get back on track. If you find yourself in this spot, simply start exercising. Don't worry about any of the other parts, just get yourself moving. No thinking. Just doing. The rest will fall into place. I find when I've put time and effort into a workout, I don't want to ruin it with trashy foods thoughtlessly eaten. I consciously eat instead. I feel good about my body when it's being exercised, and I start liking it more and more. Liking my body starts the cycle of wanting to take care of it. Take this tool for yourself for any time you need a jump start.

Refresher Course

Beyond exercise, there are a few self-care areas I find important enough to address for physical well-being. If these are broken record bits of advice, at least take it as a cue that they are important enough to be repeated again.

Recently, I heard an equally informative and horrifying TED Talk on the effects of not sleeping enough. In under twenty minutes, brain scientist Matt Walker explained that getting less sleep increases our chances of an early death. What's more, by something terrible—like a heart attack, dementia or cancer. If you're stubborn like me, impending deadly disease may not be enough to motivate you to get to bed on time, but getting fat will. A great way I can guarantee myself to overeat all day is to not get enough sleep the night before. I lose all resolve when I'm sleep-deprived, bemoaning, "I'm too tired to care," as I reach for a second pack of Little Debbie Swiss Rolls instead of going to the gym. By the way, there are two rolls in one package, so two packages is... you know, basically how one gains weight instead of loses it. Let's take a hint from *Sleeping Beauty* and get some serious snooze on.

Other than sleep, a healthy habit I have struggled with is drinking water. Actually, "struggle" is putting it a bit lightly. I used to recoil at a glass of water. I think it's because, as an anorexic teenager, I flooded my body so profusely with it, in an effort to not eat anything, that I still associate it with the painful misery of perpetual starvation. Do you see a pattern yet? Stuck on an old way of thinking. Resistance. Struggle. I needed to stop resisting water to make drinking it not feel like some sort of penance. Instead of telling myself I had to drink water or else, I gave myself permission to not have to drink it. My body was able to take over from there, signaling when it needs water by getting thirsty. This route makes drinking water easy and natural, and I find myself pouring a glass more often than I used to.

The only water I will myself to drink is when I want to curb my appetite a bit. Once in a blue moon when hunger strikes, I will want to hold off on eating, so I down a glass of water to appease my stomach. For example, if I have been looking forward to an exquisite dinner-out experience, but my belly is rumbling while I'm getting ready. I don't want to eat anything yet, so I opt for a glass of water. Other times, after I've had what I know is plenty to eat, my stomach doesn't always seem to get it and is still rumbling. A big glass of water is usually the fix.

Since each one of us is so tremendously unique and different, I would be silly to suggest some standard amount any one person should intake per day. I don't think doctors or scientists really know either. Your size, metabolism, exercise habits and what you eat or drink surely make a difference in the water you need. Therefore, my suggestion on staying hydrated is the same as that for eating and exercise. Let your body let you know.

You-ness

Above all, I hope that this process of finding what your body needs, in a way that is true to you, will help you propel a journey of finding your whole self. My issues with eating and body image were so in the way of understanding my true state of being. My try identity. My me-ness. I had to address the destructive thinking to finally get there. I truly believed that thin was the answer to happiness, which is why I put everything I had into attaining that. Everything else in life could go to poop as long as I was skinny. I would tell myself the message like, "Sure, I'm a hard-working boss lady but what does that matter if I'm fat?"

Know who you are and flip-flop these statements. Now my weight and shape don't dictate my self-worth. My messages sound more like, "I adore being an uber-feminine girly girl and I have a cute, wiggly bit of a belly," or "I am kind, empathetic and thoughtful and it's perfectly okay that I'm out of shape right now."

I implore you to take the time to discover and nurture the you that's you, no matter what body you have. In fact, it may very well be the you who was always there before you started down the path of self-hatred, sparked by not liking your looks. Your personal message may sound like, "I always look on the bright side," or "I love that I'm adventurous," or "Learning is my hobby," instead of "I'm such a chunk," or "I have three chins," or "My pants don't fit. Therefore, my life is over."

You deserve the kind, gentle, livable lifestyle of thinner bliss. Knowing yourself leads to loving yourself, and loving yourself leads to caring for yourself. That is fundamental for not only weight loss, but also, a beautiful life.

Summary of Tools

- Exercise! Yeah!
- Do the exercise that makes you feel fit and challenged.
- Don't worry about getting back to the exercise you "used to" do.
- Adjust your workouts to accommodate life

changes.
- Allow yourself to have different phases of exercise.
- Don't think just do.
- Set workout goals as needed.
- Make little additions of activity regularly.
- Feel your balance for pushing to get results and avoiding burn-outs.
- If you need a jump start, simply begin with exercising.
- Sleep, beautiful sleep.
- Drink the water your body wants.
- Get to know your true, whole self.

Comprehensive Summary of Tools

Section 1:
Change Your Mind Before Your Body

- Love your body exactly the way it is now.
- Wear clothes you look and feel your best in now.
- Make a visual aid of your style ideas.
- Find a fashion icon with a style you can model.
- Get rid of all clothes that do not properly fit you.
- Use one piece of slightly smaller clothing to gauge your weight loss progress, every

few weeks.

- Do not weigh yourself.
- Flaunt your finest physical asset(s).
- Indulge in beauty treatments.
- Believe you are already the size, shape and weight you want to be.

Section 2:
The Only Rule You'll Ever Need for Eating

- Eat whatever you want.
- Trust your body.
- Pay attention to what your body wants and doesn't want.
- Experience well-made, high quality, really good food.
- Cook for yourself.
- Enjoy your food.
- Put your food down between bites.

- Remove your desired portion of food from the original container.
- Serve your food with a nice presentation.
- Do not have distractions while you are eating.
- You do not need to finish everything on your plate.
- Enjoy drinks just like you enjoy your food.

Section 3:
Weight-Life Balance

- Avoid deprivation.
- Accept your hunger as a natural signal to enjoy eating.
- Offset the indulgences you eat with small food and beverage cuts and additional exercise.
- Make small, manageable cuts in your food

and drink intake, as you go along the day.
- Ask yourself, "Can I live without it?"
- Substitute food and drinks with leaner options, where plausible.
- Manage your hunger so it does not overtake your eating.

Section 4:
Exercise and Other Good-For-You Stuff

- Exercise! Yeah!
- Do the exercise that makes you feel fit and challenged.
- Don't worry about getting back to the exercise you "used to" do.
- Adjust your workouts to accommodate life changes.
- Allow yourself to have different phases of exercise.

- Don't think just do.
- Set workout goals as needed.
- Make little additions of activity regularly.
- Feel your balance for pushing to get results and avoiding burn-outs.
- If you need a jump start, simply begin with exercising.
- Sleep, beautiful sleep.
- Drink the water your body wants.
- Get to know your true, whole self.

www.ingramcontent.com/pod-product-compliance
Lightning Source LLC
Chambersburg PA
CBHW021412290426
44108CB00010B/497